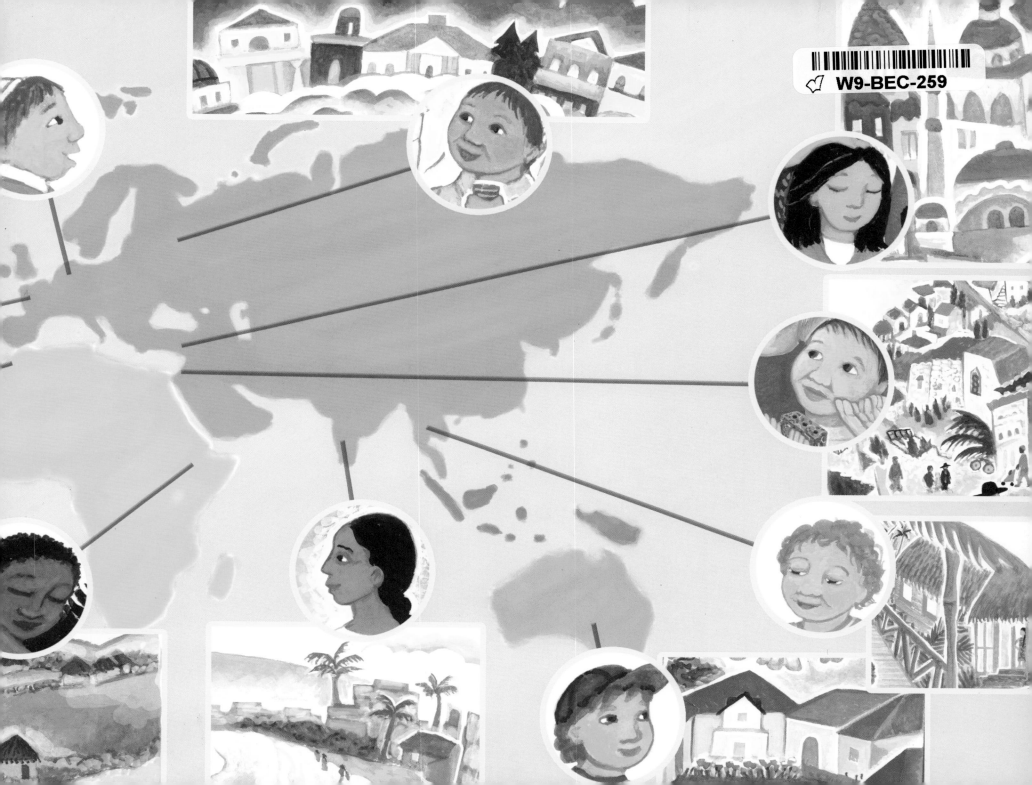

Around the World in One Shabbat

Jewish People Celebrate the Sabbath Together

Durga Yael Bernhard

JEWISH LIGHTS Publishing

Woodstock, Vermont

Author's Note for Parents & Teachers

The story of creation is told all over the world. In the Hebrew Bible, the Sabbath is woven into the book of Genesis, or Creation. When dark and light, sea and land, earth and sky, plants and trees, sun and moon, fish, birds, animals, people, and all the things of the world were complete, God drew a breath and rested. A sanctuary in time was created: Shabbat.

The Sabbath is observed in different ways by different people. The Hebrew word *Shabbat,* the Yiddish word *Shabbos,* or the English term *Sabbath* all mean "rest." For Jewish people everywhere, it is when the sun sets each Friday evening that the Sabbath begins. In six days, the Torah tells us, God created the world, and on the seventh day God rested, setting this day apart forever as holy time. From sundown to sundown, Jews all over the world remember the fourth commandment handed down to them by their ancestors—*Remember the Sabbath and keep it holy*—and reenact the story of Creation by stopping their weekly labors. We replenish our souls with blessings, prayers, study, peaceful rest, good food, the beauty of nature, and the company of family and friends. You, too, are invited to light the Sabbath candles, to share the blessings, and to celebrate life!

Happy are we,
how fortunate our people,
how pleasing our lives,
how lovely our traditions!
Happy are we
to be at rest on the seventh day,
and thus it is written in our Torah:

Let Israel's descendents keep and remember Shabbat
throughout all time
as an everlasting promise.

For all the Jewish people,
Shabbat shall be a sign eternally,
for in six days the Creator
made the heavens and the earth,
and on the seventh day God ceased,
and drew a breath of rest.

—*Kedushat Hayom* (The Holiness of the Day)

The sun is not yet up over the rooftops of Jerusalem, but Avi doesn't mind waking up early. As every Friday morning, today is the beginning of a special day. Avi dresses quickly and finds his grandma, *Savta*, and his sister, Rachel, waiting for him by the door. *Savta* takes his hand, and soon Avi's feet are moving quickly to keep up with hers on the sidewalk. Even from blocks away, the sounds of the *Machane Yehudah* market can be heard as hundreds of people shop for the weekly holiday of Shabbat.

Soon the sights and smells of the market are all around Avi and Rachel. Shiny loaves of challah, spicy *bourekas*, pickled olives, sweet halva, fresh greens, and fragrant flowers fill their senses. But *Savta* does not let them linger. She chooses quickly, her fingers finding the choicest chicken and freshest vegetables for the Sabbath meal. Avi and Rachel know that after a hard week of work and school, the seventh day is holy time, and the Sabbath table must have only the best food. *Savta* even lets Avi choose a shiny pomegranate, and buys it for him. He hides the special fruit in his jacket like a secret, but *Savta* sees it, and says Avi has a pomegranate for a heart!

In Buenos Aires, Argentina, the sun is already high in the sky when Alicia wakes from her nap.

Laughter comes from the kitchen as Alicia's sister and her friend are kneading challah dough.

Papa is home from work early to prepare for the Sabbath. He empties his pockets, dropping

a coin in Alicia's *tzedakah* box, and leaves his wallet and keys in a special drawer until

after the day of rest. Then he gets busy helping to wash and clean the house.

Everyone is preparing for a special guest who is

about to arrive: it is an invisible guest, the

Sabbath bride, the special feeling that fills

the house every Friday at sundown. Alicia

will not see it, but she knows it will be there.

Alicia helps her sister roll the bread dough

into long strands. Carefully they weave the

strands together to make a braided loaf.

Soon Alicia will have a bath and then, like a

bride herself, she will put on her special white

blouse for Shabbat!

In Melbourne, Australia, Aaron walks home from school on Friday afternoon with his best friend, Ben. They pass the synagogue, and Aaron waves goodbye and runs up the path to his house. Inside, his cousins have arrived with fresh-cut flowers for the Sabbath table. They spread out their special Shabbat tablecloth, and bring out the family's best silver, prettiest glasses, and fanciest napkins. Aaron puts new candles in the Shabbat candlesticks. In the kitchen, Mother is slicing leeks and peeling potatoes, and Dad is trimming meat. Their dog, Latka, begs for scraps, but Dad shoos him away—like the rest of the family, he will have to wait for the special Shabbat meal. Aaron takes Latka for a walk before the sun goes down. Outside, he meets a neighbor who hands him a package of homemade cookies, a special gift for the Sabbath. The whole neighborhood is brimming with excitement as everyone gets ready for Shabbat!

9

Praised are You, Adonai, our God, Ruler of the universe, who made us holy through Your commandments, and commanded us to kindle the Shabbat lights.

בָּרוּךְ אַתָּה יְיָ, אֱלֹהֵינוּ מֶלֶךְ הָעוֹלָם, אֲשֶׁר קִדְּשָׁנוּ בְּמִצְוֹתָיו וְצִוָּנוּ לְהַדְלִיק נֵר שֶׁל שַׁבָּת.

10

The red roofs of Istanbul, Turkey, glow in the setting sun as Leyla puts her school

books away. She quickly brushes her hair, and runs downstairs as her

brother, David, arrives home with fresh roses for the Sabbath

table. Brother and sister hurry to join the family

around the table to welcome the Sabbath. Leyla's

mother covers her head with a beautiful

embroidered cloth. Her father, *Abba*, puts on

his special *kippa* and his favorite slippers that he

wears only on Shabbat. *Ima* lights the two candles—one

to remember, and one to guard the Sabbath—then closes her eyes and covers her face with

her hands, singing the blessing softly. A quiet hush falls over the house as everyone gazes

at the flickering candlelight. Then *Ima* and *Abba* place their hands gently on their

children's heads. Together they bless them, wishing them lives of good health, joy, and peace.

Now the family stands quietly. The golden rays of sunset bring a feeling of peace as Shabbat

begins. Every Friday, no matter how hard she has worked in school or how many chores she has done,

Leyla knows Shabbat will be there, surrounding her family with peace.

May Adonai bless you יְבָרֶכְךָ יְיָ וְיִשְׁמְרֶךָ. and guard you.

Praised are you, Adonai, our God, בָּרוּךְ אַתָּה יְיָ

Ruler of the universe, Creator of the fruit of the vine. אֱלֹהֵינוּ מֶלֶךְ

הָעוֹלָם, בּוֹרֵא פְּרִי הַגָּפֶן.

12

Far away in St. Petersburg, Russia, twilight fills the sky with purple and blue. Inside the warm house, Isaac climbs onto his grandfather *Zayde*'s lap. Papa pours the wine for the Kiddush blessing. Then he says *"L'chaim!"* as he lifts the Kiddush cup over the candles glowing with the light of Shabbat. Isaac takes a sip of sweet grape juice from his own cup. Now the *zemirot*, the special songs of Shabbat, begin. Mama's voice always starts softly with *Shalom Aleichem*. Then Isaac's *Zayde* joins in with his big voice, clapping his hands above his head and bouncing Isaac on his knee. Soon everyone is singing and stomping their feet under the table with the joy of Shabbat. Isaac grabs a spoon and taps it on the edge of the table. In six days God created the world and now another week is over. Like Jews everywhere, Isaac is glad he is not a slave like his ancestors were a long time ago in Egypt. He knows his own family has worked hard for their freedom. And he knows that on Shabbat, it is time to celebrate the goodness of life!

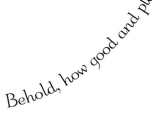

Behold, how good and pleasant it is for brethren to dwell together in unity.

הִנֵּה מַה־טּוֹב וּמַה־נָּעִים שֶׁבֶת אַחִים גַּם־יָחַד.

14

The moon is just beginning to rise over the south of France as people gather for Friday evening *Kabbalat Shabbat*. Simone's mother fixes a circle of white lace to Simone's hair, then together they follow the crowd into the synagogue. *"Shabbat Shalom,"* everyone says to wish each other a peaceful Sabbath. Simone sits on her mother's lap on the long wooden benches. Then everyone rises to face the door, and sings *Lecha Dodi* to welcome the Sabbath bride. Simone gazes up at the sparkling chandeliers that hang from the ceiling. She can almost see the angels of Shabbat floating among the lights. She listens to the cantor's voice and looks around at all the familiar faces. Across the aisle Simone sees her friend Maurice. Maurice's family often comes to Simone's house to share the Sabbath meal.

Simone waves at Maurice, and he waves back. They both know there will be plenty of desserts tonight—maybe chocolate éclairs or Simone's favorite lemon tarts. Shabbat is a time for special friends and special treats!

בָּרוּךְ אַתָּה יְיָ, אֱלֹהֵינוּ מֶלֶךְ הָעוֹלָם, הַמּוֹצִיא לֶחֶם מִן הָאָרֶץ.

Praised are you, Adonai, our God, Ruler of the universe, who brings forth bread from the earth.

16

Nestled in the fields of New England, the synagogue is full of activity. Ducking under arms and between bodies, Becka makes her way to the center of the room where everyone gathers for the *Hamotzi* blessing. Now the rabbi lifts two loaves of challah above the crowd. Becka stands on her tippy toes to reach the warm bread, just barely touching it with her fingertips. As she does so, she feels hands on her shoulders as other people join in. Everyone touches someone who is touching the challah—or someone who is touching someone who is touching the challah—until all the people are connected to the two *challot*. Then all voices join together to bless the Sabbath bread. Becka waits to hear "Amen," then digs her fingers into the soft loaf, tearing off a big piece. She breaks this in half and passes both pieces to reaching hands, grabbing a shred for herself as it disappears. Everyone smiles as they taste the blessing of freshly baked bread and the feeling of happiness that is *Oneg Shabbat*.

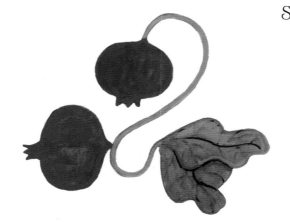

17

On Saturday morning, Avraham wakes as always to the sound of roosters calling, but even before he opens his eyes, he knows this day is different. The brown hills of Ethiopia are the same outside his window, but somehow the world feels new. Avraham does not have to get up early today to gather firewood. He does not have to hurry off to school. Avraham dresses slowly, and finds his parents sitting in the shade of the *wanza* tree. His mother does not have to roast coffee beans this morning, and his father does not have to work at the market. Even the family's donkey will not have to carry heavy sacks of fava beans. The whole world seems to be wrapped in *menuhah*, the special rest of Shabbat. Avraham looks out at the land that stretches away to the north, toward Israel. He thinks of his older brother and sister who are soldiers there. He knows that far away, his relatives are also having a quiet Sabbath morning. Like him, they will soon walk to synagogue to share the morning blessings.

In the big new synagogue in Germany, Joseph holds his father's hand and plays with the fringes on his prayer shawl. Today is his brother's bar mitzvah, and the family sits in the front row. When the rabbi takes the big Torah scrolls from the ark and hands them to Joseph's brother, Joseph joins the parade of people who follow him around the room. Everyone sings and smiles at Joseph and his brother. They reach out to touch the Torah with their *tallit* fringes or prayer books. Joseph's voice

blends with all the voices around him as everyone sings the Hebrew words that are being sung by Jews everywhere on this sacred day of Shabbat. He claps his hands for all the good things God created in the world, especially music! Most of all, he claps his hands for the Torah, the teachings and stories that promise to fill him with goodness and learning for all the days of his life. Like his older brother, someday Joseph will be big enough to carry the Torah scrolls, and to chant the words that were written so long ago.

The first snowflakes are falling on the bare trees of Montreal, Canada, as Miriam walks home from synagogue with her family through the park. Her great grandmother, Nana Elsa, walks slowly, but no one is in a rush. On Shabbat, there is plenty of time to stop on the bridge and throw sticks in the stream. Nana tells about the bridges of Amsterdam that she ran over as a girl, as Miriam watches a leaf twirl to the ground. She sees a squirrel gathering nuts in a tree, and notices where a woodpecker has made holes in a tree trunk. She skips ahead, then stops to pick up a special rock and puts it in her pocket. She can still hear the songs of Shabbat inside her head. All around her, the day seems to be gently smiling. Miriam wishes every day could be Shabbat. Nana says it is a taste of a time to come that is promised by the prophet Eliyahu, when all the world will be at peace.

24

Praised are you, Adonai, our God, Ruler of the universe, who made us holy through Your commandments, and commanded us concerning the washing of hands.

עַל נְטִילַת יָדָיִם.

וְצִוָּנוּ ... אֲשֶׁר קִדְּשָׁנוּ בְּמִצְוֹתָיו

בָּרוּךְ אַתָּה יְיָ אֱלֹהֵינוּ מֶלֶךְ הָעוֹלָם,

The smell of warm bread and spices spreads through the house in Casablanca, Morocco. Hayyim is glad the Shabbat lunch was prepared the day before. He is hungry, and everything smells good. A pitcher of water and a bowl are passed around the table. Hayyim and his brother say the blessing for the washing of hands. Now plates of chickpea salad, couscous, and harissa are passed around. Hayyim's parents smile and laugh as they relax and eat. His uncle talks about the weekly Torah portion. His aunt has news from relatives in faraway France and Israel. Hayyim dips spicy fish balls in lemon sauce and listens. He does not want the Sabbath meal to end. But soon it is time to say the blessing to give thanks for the food they have eaten. Hayyim's belly is full of good food, and his soul is full with the blessings and stories of Shabbat.

Praised are You, Adonai, Our God, Ruler of the universe, who feeds the whole world with goodness, kindness, and compassion.

בָּרוּךְ אַתָּה יְיָ אֱלֹהֵינוּ מֶלֶךְ הָעוֹלָם, הַזָּן אֶת־הָעוֹלָם כֻּלּוֹ בְּטוּבוֹ בְּחֵן בְּחֶסֶד וּבְרַחֲמִים.

25

It's a drizzly afternoon in Thailand, Dani's favorite kind of weather for Shabbat. Dani's friend Nathan from California knocks on the door. The two boys take out Dani's toy ark, colored animals, and cut-out figures of Noah, his family, and animals of every color. They spread them out on the floor, pretending the rug is a great ocean. On Shabbat, Dani and Nathan can play all afternoon. Everyone in the family relaxes. Dani's grandparents call from Tel Aviv to say "Good Shabbos," but his father has fallen asleep in the hammock. Dani's big sister, Tamar, takes the call, then goes back to reading her book. His mother is out visiting friends from London who she met on the beach. Later, they will join Dani's family for *Havdalah*. Now the rain stops, and the boys take a bowl of food scraps outside to feed the neighbor's baby goat. It is a day of sharing and rest for people and animals, rich and poor, young and old, family and friends.

The sun is hot along the west coast of India, but the late afternoon breeze is cool on the beach. Zipporah spreads a colorful cloth under a tall palm tree. It is a special Shabbat tablecloth, decorated with a design of figs and pomegranates, dates and olives, wheat, barley, and grapes: all the foods of the ancient Holy Land where Zipporah's family came from long ago. Zipporah sits with her family and eats curried lentils and rice left over from the Sabbath lunch. Even when the food is cold, a special spice makes it taste especially good. It is not a spice you can buy in the market or make yourself. It is the magic spice of Shabbat. After the meal, Zipporah's

parents take a walk together down the beach, holding hands. *Savta*, her grandmother, dozes with her back to the tree. Zipporah listens to the waves and chews on a coconut date roll while her little brother plays in the sand. The sky begins to turn pink as the sun drops toward the horizon. The family lingers in their day of rest, for soon Shabbat will be over and a new and busy week will begin.

Praised are You, Adonai, our God, Ruler of the universe, who creates all kinds of spices ... who distinguishes between Shabbat and the six days of work.

בָּרוּךְ אַתָּה יְיָ, אֱלֹהֵינוּ מֶלֶךְ הָעוֹלָם, בּוֹרֵא מִינֵי בְשָׂמִים ... הַמַּבְדִּיל בֵּין יוֹם הַשְּׁבִיעִי לְשֵׁשֶׁת יְמֵי הַמַּעֲשֶׂה.

Jerusalem is quiet as the sun begins to set. Avi and Rachel walk home with their family from the Kotel, the ancient stone wall where the temples of Solomon and Herod were built. As they leave the old city, no buses clog the streets and all the stores are closed for Shabbat. By the time they arrive home, Avi can already count the first three stars in the sky, marking the end of Shabbat. He finds the little painted box of spices, and *Savta* fills it with the fresh herbs they bought at the market the day before. *Ima* calls Avi's sister, Rachel, and her friend Ephraim to join the family for *Havdalah*. *Abba* fills the Kiddush cup with wine, and *Ima* lights the braided *Havdalah* candle that is lit at the end of Shabbat. Avi holds the little box under his nose as the final Sabbath *brachah* is spoken. He knows that all over the world, children like him are smelling fragrant herbs and spices to remember the sweetness of Shabbat. Everyone holds their hands toward the light, watching the shadows of their fingers. Then *Ima* plunges the candle into the cup of wine and puts it out. "*Shavua tov,*" she says—a good week!—and kisses all the children. Avi feels a little sad as the special Sabbath day comes to an end. But he is already looking forward to next Friday, when his family will stop to rest, to welcome Shabbat all over again, and to celebrate the special day with Jewish people around the world.

ליוני

For Jonathan,
who made this book possible in so many ways,
and who walked the streets of Jerusalem with me on Erev Shabbat,
passing candlelit windows
and listening to the sounds
of laughter and zemirot.

Acknowledgments

The author wishes to gratefully acknowledge the following people who supported the creation of this book: Jonathan Follender, Rabbi Naftali Haleva, Gwendolyn Tapper, Stuart M. Matlins, Emily Wichland, Ronnie Herman, Julie Makowsky, Neslihan Ulus, Meg Gerson, Laurie Schwartz, Chris Countryman, Marie Claire Foss, Sharon Burns Leader, Sage Rivka Bernhard, Karen Levine; and special thanks to Rabbi Jonathan Kligler for his tireless assistance with research.

Around the World in One Shabbat:
Jewish People Celebrate the Sabbath Together

2011 Hardcover Edition, First Printing
© 2011 by Durga Yael Bernhard

Kedushat Hayom inspired by the presentation in *Kol Haneshemah*, 3rd Edition, The Reconstructionist Press.

Library of Congress
Cataloging-in-Publication Data
Bernhard, Durga.
Around the world in one Shabbat : Jewish people celebrate the Sabbath together /
Durga Yael Bernhard. — 2011 hardcover ed.
p. cm.
ISBN 978-1-58023-433-7 (hardcover)
1. Sabbath—Juvenile literature. I. Title.
BM685.B425 2011
296.4'1—dc22

2010041803

10 9 8 7 6 5 4 3 2 1
Manufactured in China
Jacket design: Durga Yael Bernhard and Tim Holtz
Jacket and interior art: Durga Yael Bernhard

Published by Jewish Lights Publishing
A Division of Longhill Partners, Inc.
Sunset Farm Offices, Route 4, P.O. Box 237
Woodstock, VT 05091
Tel: (802) 457-4000   Fax: (802) 457-4004
www.jewishlights.com

Glossary

Abba Hebrew for "father"

angel from the Hebrew Bible, a messenger from God

bar/bat mitzvah Hebrew for "son or daughter of the *mitzvot*," or commandments of the Torah; a ceremony marking a child reaching the age of adult religious responsibility

bourekas a Middle Eastern puff pastry filled with various fillings such as meat, cheese, spinach, or eggplant

brachah Hebrew for "blessing"; words spoken formally to praise, to make something sacred, or to ask for divine protection

challah (pl., *challot*) Hebrew name of a special braided bread eaten on Shabbat

couscous semolina, the starchy part of wheat, cooked and eaten like pasta, often with a sauce made from meat and vegetables

halva a Middle Eastern dessert made from sesame seed butter

harissa a North African spicy hot red sauce or chili paste

Havdalah Hebrew for "separation"; a special ceremony on Saturday evening to divide Shabbat from the beginning of the week

Ima Hebrew for "mother"

Kabbalat Shabbat Hebrew for "welcoming Shabbat"; a ceremony done on Friday evening as Shabbat begins

Kiddush the Hebrew name for the blessing said over wine on Shabbat and other Jewish holidays to emphasize the holiness of the day

kippa Hebrew word for a small cap worn as a sign of reverence for God; traditionally worn by men only, today worn in some places by women, too; *yarmulke* in Yiddish

L'chaim Hebrew expression "to life!," usually said in a toast

Machane Yehudah a covered outdoor marketplace in Jerusalem; also called the "Shuk" (shook)

menuhah Hebrew word for the special rest of Shabbat; a feeling of contentment

Oneg Shabbat Hebrew for "Joy of the Sabbath"; an informal gathering for food and conversation after Shabbat services

parshah Hebrew for "portion"; the weekly portion of the Torah that is read by Jews everywhere as part of a yearly cycle, and discussed on Shabbat

Savta Hebrew for "grandmother"

Shabbat Hebrew for "rest"; the traditional day on which no work is to be done

tallit Hebrew word for a prayer shawl with special fringes, or *tzitzit*, attached to the corners as a reminder of the commandments

Torah Hebrew for "teaching"; the Hebrew Bible or Five Books of Moses, written by hand on a scroll or printed as bound books

Torah ark Holy Ark, or *Aron Hakodesh* in Hebrew; a special cabinet where Torah scrolls are stored in a synagogue

tzedakah box a special box where money for charity, or *tzedakah*, is collected

Zayde Yiddish for "grandfather"

zemirot special songs of Shabbat

Award-Winning Children's Books from Jewish Lights

Adam & Eve's First Sunset
God's New Day
by Sandy Eisenberg Sasso
Illustrations by Joani Keller Rothenberg
Explores fear and hope, faith and gratitude, in a way that kids will understand.
For ages 4 & up. 9 x 12, 32 pp, Full-color illus., HC, 978-1-58023-177-0 $17.95
Also available—a board book for kids 0–4:
Adam & Eve's New Day 978-1-59473-205-8 $7.99
(SkyLight Paths)

Because Nothing Looks Like God
by Lawrence Kushner and Karen Kushner
Illustrations by Dawn W. Majewski
Lights children's creativity and shows how God is with us every day, in every way. Invites parents and children to explore, together, the questions we all have about God, no matter what our age.
For ages 4 & up. 11 x 8½, 32 pp, Full-color illus., HC, 978-1-58023-092-6 $17.99
Also Available: Teacher's Guide by Karen Kushner:
For ages 5–8. 8½ x 11, 22 pp, PB, 978-1-58023-140-4 $6.95

But God Remembered
Stories of Women from Creation to the Promised Land
by Sandy Eisenberg Sasso
Illustrations by Bethanne Andersen
Four different stories of women briefly mentioned in biblical tradition and religious texts, but never explored.
For ages 8 & up. 9 x 12, 32 pp, Full-color illus., Quality PB, 978-1-58023-372-9 $8.99

The 11th Commandment
Wisdom from Our Children
by The Children of America
"If there were an Eleventh Commandment, what would it be?" Children of many religious denominations across America answer this question—in their own drawings and words—in this inspiring book.
For all ages. 8 x 10, 48 pp, Full-color illus., HC, 978-1-879045-46-0 $16.95

Cain & Abel
Finding the Fruits of Peace
by Sandy Eisenberg Sasso
Illustrations by Joani Keller Rothenberg
A beautiful recasting of the biblical tale. A spiritual conversation-starter about anger and how to deal with it, for parents and children to share.
Ages 5 & up. 9 x 12, 32 pp, Full-color illus., HC, 978-1-58023-123-7 $16.95

For Heaven's Sake
by Sandy Eisenberg Sasso
Illustrations by Kathryn Kunz Finney
Isaiah, a young boy, searches for heaven and learns that it is often found in the places where you least expect it.
For ages 4 & up. 9 x 12, 32 pp, Full-color illus., HC, 978-1-58023-054-4 $16.95

God in Between
by Sandy Eisenberg Sasso
Illustrations by Sally Sweetland
If you wanted to find God, where would you look? Teaches that God can be found where we are.
For ages 4 & up. 9 x 12, 32 pp, Full-color illus., HC, 978-1-879045-86-6 $16.95

God Said Amen
by Sandy Eisenberg Sasso
Illustrations by Avi Katz
A stubborn Prince and Princess show children and adults how self-centered actions affect the people around us, and how by working together we can work with God—to create a better world.
For ages 4 & up. 9 x 12, 32 pp, Full-color illus., HC, 978-1-58023-080-3 $16.95

God's Paintbrush
Special 10th Anniversary Edition
by Sandy Eisenberg Sasso
Illustrations by Annette Compton
Invites children of all faiths and backgrounds to encounter God openly through moments in their own lives—and help the adults who love them to be a part of that encounter.
For ages 4 & up. 11 x 8½, 32 pp, Full-color illus., HC, 978-1-58023-195-4 $17.95
Also available—a board book version for kids 0–4:
I Am God's Paintbrush 978-1-59473-265-2 $7.99
(SkyLight Paths)

God's Paintbrush Celebration Kit
A Spiritual Activity Kit for Teachers and Students of All Faiths, All Backgrounds
by Sandy Eisenberg Sasso & Rev. Donald Schmidt
Illustrations by Annette Compton
With delightful illustrations and activity sheets to encourage discussion, this indispensable, completely nonsectarian teaching tool is designed for all religious education settings.
Five sessions for eight children ages 5–8.
9 x 12, 40 Full-color activity sheets and teacher folder, 978-1-58023-050-6 $21.95